EMMANUEL JOSEPH

The Recipe for Connection, How Food, Society, and Robots Redefine Human Interaction

Copyright © 2025 by Emmanuel Joseph

All rights reserved. No part of this publication may be reproduced, stored or transmitted in any form or by any means, electronic, mechanical, photocopying, recording, scanning, or otherwise without written permission from the publisher. It is illegal to copy this book, post it to a website, or distribute it by any other means without permission.

First edition

This book was professionally typeset on Reedsy.
Find out more at reedsy.com

Contents

1	Chapter 1: Introduction to the Power of Food	1
2	Chapter 2: The Social Fabric of Dining	3
3	Chapter 3: The Role of Food in Cultural Exchange	5
4	Chapter 4: The Intersection of Food and Technology	7
5	Chapter 5: Robots in the Kitchen	9
6	Chapter 6: Food and Artificial Intelligence	11
7	Chapter 7: The Evolution of Food Culture	13
8	Chapter 8: Food as a Medium for Storytelling	15
9	Chapter 9: The Future of Dining Experiences	17
10	Chapter 10: The Role of Food in Community Building	19
11	Chapter 11: Food and Emotional Well-being	21
12	Chapter 12: Conclusion: Redefining Human Interaction Through...	23
13	Chapter 13: The Role of Food in Education	25
14	Chapter 14: Food and Social Justice	27
15	Chapter 15: The Impact of Food on Environmental...	29
16	Chapter 16: The Role of Food in Health and Wellness	31
17	Chapter 17: The Future of Food and Society	33

1

Chapter 1: Introduction to the Power of Food

The universal language of food transcends geographical, cultural, and social barriers. It's a means of expression, a tool for communication, and a bridge that connects people across different walks of life. From the simplest home-cooked meals to extravagant feasts, food plays a pivotal role in human society. Its power goes beyond sustenance; it fosters relationships, evokes memories, and creates shared experiences that strengthen bonds. In this chapter, we explore how food's transformative power has shaped human interaction throughout history.

Food has always been central to cultural identity and social structures. Traditional recipes passed down through generations carry stories, wisdom, and a sense of belonging. These culinary practices not only preserve heritage but also bring people together during communal gatherings, festivals, and celebrations. The act of sharing a meal embodies hospitality, generosity, and unity, reinforcing the social fabric of communities.

Moreover, the rise of the global food movement has further highlighted food's role in connecting diverse populations. Farmers' markets, food festivals, and culinary tourism have become popular avenues for cultural exchange and appreciation. These interactions foster mutual understanding and respect, breaking down prejudices and fostering a sense of global citizenship. Food has the unique ability to transcend language barriers, allowing people to connect on a deeper, more visceral level.

In modern society, the relationship between food and technology is rapidly evolving. From farm-to-table initiatives to innovative culinary techniques, advancements in technology have revolutionized the way we produce, prepare, and consume food. This chapter sets the stage for exploring how these technological advancements, coupled with the timeless power of food, are redefining human interaction in the digital age.

2

Chapter 2: The Social Fabric of Dining

Dining has always been a social activity that fosters connections and strengthens relationships. The act of sharing a meal creates a sense of camaraderie and belonging, whether it's a family dinner, a business lunch, or a casual gathering with friends. In this chapter, we delve into the social dynamics of dining and how it has evolved over time.

Throughout history, communal dining has been a cornerstone of human society. Ancient civilizations held elaborate feasts to celebrate victories, honor deities, and mark significant life events. These gatherings provided an opportunity for individuals to bond, share stories, and strengthen social ties. The tradition of communal dining continues today, with holidays, weddings, and other special occasions often centered around a shared meal.

In contemporary society, the way we dine has undergone significant changes. The rise of fast food and convenience dining has altered traditional meal structures, with many families eating on the go or in front of screens. However, the desire for meaningful connections remains strong. The resurgence of supper clubs, communal tables in restaurants, and pop-up dining experiences reflect a growing trend towards reclaiming the social aspect of dining. These experiences encourage conversation, interaction, and the forging of new relationships.

The digital age has also introduced new dimensions to dining. Virtual dinner parties, online cooking classes, and social media food communities have emerged as innovative ways to connect with others through food. These platforms enable individuals to share recipes, culinary tips, and food-related experiences, fostering a sense of community even in the absence of physical proximity. The integration of technology into dining experiences highlights the evolving nature of human interaction in the modern world.

3

Chapter 3: The Role of Food in Cultural Exchange

Food is a powerful medium for cultural exchange, allowing people to explore and appreciate the diversity of human traditions and practices. In this chapter, we examine how food facilitates cross-cultural understanding and promotes global unity.

Culinary traditions are deeply rooted in cultural heritage, reflecting the history, geography, and values of a community. By sharing these traditions, individuals can gain insights into the lives and experiences of others. Food festivals, international food markets, and cultural exchange programs provide opportunities for people to sample dishes from around the world and learn about the customs and rituals associated with them. These experiences foster a sense of curiosity, respect, and appreciation for different cultures.

The globalization of cuisine has also played a significant role in cultural exchange. The widespread availability of international ingredients and the popularity of ethnic restaurants have introduced people to new flavors and cooking techniques. This culinary cross-pollination has led to the creation of fusion dishes that blend elements from different culinary traditions, symbolizing the interconnectedness of the modern world. Food has become a conduit for cultural diffusion, breaking down barriers and promoting a sense of global interconnectedness.

In addition to cultural exchange, food also serves as a tool for diplomacy and conflict resolution. Culinary diplomacy, also known as gastrodiplomacy, involves using food as a means of fostering dialogue and building bridges between nations. Diplomatic events, state dinners, and international culinary initiatives have demonstrated the power of food to facilitate understanding and cooperation. By sharing a meal, individuals can find common ground, transcend differences, and work towards mutual goals.

4

Chapter 4: The Intersection of Food and Technology

Technology has revolutionized the food industry, transforming the way we produce, prepare, and consume food. In this chapter, we explore the intersection of food and technology and its impact on human interaction.

Advancements in agricultural technology have significantly increased food production and efficiency. Precision farming, vertical farming, and genetically modified organisms (GMOs) are just a few examples of how technology has improved crop yields and reduced environmental impact. These innovations have enabled farmers to meet the growing demand for food, ensuring that communities around the world have access to nutritious and affordable sustenance. The availability of diverse ingredients has also enriched culinary practices, allowing for greater experimentation and creativity in the kitchen.

The rise of food delivery apps and online grocery services has redefined convenience in the modern world. With just a few taps on a smartphone, individuals can have a wide array of dishes delivered to their doorstep or order groceries with ease. This shift has not only changed consumer behavior but also created new opportunities for social interaction. Virtual dinner parties, where friends and family order the same meal and dine together via video call, have become a popular way to stay connected despite physical distance. These digital dining experiences demonstrate how technology can enhance social bonds in the age of convenience.

Moreover, technology has revolutionized the culinary arts, introducing new techniques and tools that push the boundaries of gastronomy. Molecular gastronomy, 3D food printing, and smart kitchen appliances are just a few examples of how technology has enabled chefs and home cooks to experiment with new flavors, textures, and presentations. These innovations have elevated the dining experience, turning meals into multisensory events that captivate and engage diners. The fusion of technology and culinary creativity highlights the limitless possibilities for redefining human interaction through food.

5

Chapter 5: Robots in the Kitchen

The integration of robotics into the food industry has introduced new dimensions to food production, preparation, and service. In this chapter, we examine the role of robots in the kitchen and their impact on human interaction.

Robotic technology has streamlined food production processes, improving efficiency and consistency. Automated farming equipment, robotic harvesters, and precision irrigation systems have transformed agriculture, allowing farmers to manage large-scale operations with greater precision. In food processing plants, robotic systems handle tasks such as sorting, packaging, and quality control, ensuring that products meet high standards of safety and quality. These advancements have not only increased productivity but also created opportunities for collaboration between humans and robots, enhancing the overall efficiency of the food supply chain.

In commercial kitchens, robots have taken on various roles, from cooking and plating dishes to delivering food to customers. Robotic chefs, equipped with advanced sensors and algorithms, can replicate complex recipes with precision and consistency. These culinary robots work alongside human chefs, assisting with repetitive tasks and allowing them to focus on creative aspects of cooking. The collaboration between humans and robots in the kitchen has redefined the culinary landscape, blending tradition with innovation.

The introduction of robots in the kitchen has also changed the dining experience for consumers. Automated restaurants, where robots handle everything from taking orders to serving food, have emerged as novel dining destinations. These establishments offer a unique and futuristic experience, attracting curious diners who seek to explore the possibilities of robotic technology. While the absence of human servers may alter the social dynamics of dining, the novelty and efficiency of robotic service create new opportunities for interaction and engagement.

6

Chapter 6: Food and Artificial Intelligence

Artificial intelligence (AI) has become an integral part of the food industry, driving innovation and enhancing human interaction. In this chapter, we explore how AI is transforming the way we produce, prepare, and enjoy food.

AI-powered systems have revolutionized agriculture, enabling farmers to optimize crop management and improve yields. Predictive analytics, powered by AI, can forecast weather patterns, identify pest infestations, and recommend optimal planting schedules. These insights allow farmers to make informed decisions, reducing waste and maximizing productivity. AI-driven technologies, such as autonomous tractors and drones, further enhance precision farming, ensuring that resources are used efficiently and sustainably.

In the culinary world, AI is changing the way we create and experience food. Recipe recommendation algorithms analyze individual preferences and dietary restrictions to suggest personalized meal plans and recipes. AI-powered cooking assistants, such as smart kitchen appliances and voice-activated devices, provide real-time guidance and support during meal preparation. These innovations empower home cooks to experiment with new dishes and techniques, fostering creativity and culinary exploration.

Moreover, AI is enhancing the dining experience in restaurants. Chatbots and virtual assistants streamline the reservation process, provide personalized recommendations, and assist with dietary preferences. AI-driven systems analyze customer feedback and data to optimize menu offerings, ensuring that diners have a memorable and satisfying experience. The integration of AI into the dining experience highlights the potential for technology to enhance human interaction and create meaningful connections through food.

7

Chapter 7: The Evolution of Food Culture

Food culture has evolved significantly over time, influenced by societal changes, technological advancements, and global trends. In this chapter, we examine the evolution of food culture and its impact on human interaction.

The rise of the slow food movement has emphasized the importance of quality, sustainability, and ethical food practices. This cultural shift has shifted focus from fast food convenience to celebrating the artistry of food preparation and the joy of eating mindfully. This movement encourages consumers to connect with their food sources, support local producers, and savor the dining experience. The slow food philosophy promotes a deeper understanding and appreciation of culinary traditions, fostering a sense of community and shared values.

Another significant trend in food culture is the growing awareness of health and wellness. As individuals become more health-conscious, there is an increasing demand for nutritious, organic, and plant-based options. This shift has given rise to new dietary trends and culinary innovations, such as superfoods, functional foods, and alternative protein sources. Food has become a means of promoting personal well-being, with an emphasis on balanced nutrition and mindful eating.

The influence of social media on food culture cannot be overstated. Platforms like Instagram, TikTok, and YouTube have transformed the way people discover, share, and engage with food. Food influencers and content creators have built communities around their culinary passions, inspiring others to experiment with new recipes and cooking techniques. The visual appeal of food has taken center stage, with beautifully plated dishes and food photography becoming an art form in itself. Social media has democratized culinary inspiration, allowing individuals from all walks of life to showcase their creativity and connect with a global audience.

8

Chapter 8: Food as a Medium for Storytelling

Food has the power to tell stories, preserving memories and conveying emotions. In this chapter, we explore how food serves as a medium for storytelling and its impact on human connection.

Every dish has a story behind it, whether it's a family recipe passed down through generations or a new creation inspired by a personal experience. These stories add depth and meaning to the dining experience, transforming a simple meal into a narrative journey. By sharing the stories behind their dishes, chefs and home cooks create a sense of intimacy and connection with their diners. This storytelling aspect of food fosters empathy and understanding, allowing individuals to connect on a deeper, more emotional level.

Food also serves as a vehicle for preserving cultural heritage and identity. Traditional recipes and cooking techniques are often closely tied to a community's history and way of life. By documenting and sharing these culinary traditions, individuals can ensure that their cultural heritage is passed on to future generations. Food blogs, cookbooks, and culinary documentaries are just a few examples of how food stories are being preserved and shared in the digital age. These narratives celebrate the diversity of human experiences and contribute to a richer understanding of our collective history.

In addition to personal and cultural narratives, food can also convey broader social and political messages. Culinary activism, or food justice, addresses issues such as food insecurity, sustainability, and equitable access to healthy food. Chefs, farmers, and food advocates use their platforms to raise awareness and drive change, highlighting the interconnectedness of food and social justice. By engaging with these narratives, individuals can gain a deeper appreciation of the complex relationship between food and society and be inspired to take action in their own communities.

9

Chapter 9: The Future of Dining Experiences

As technology continues to evolve, the future of dining experiences holds exciting possibilities. In this chapter, we explore emerging trends and innovations that will shape the way we dine and connect with others.

One of the most significant trends in the future of dining is the rise of immersive and multisensory experiences. Restaurants and dining establishments are incorporating elements such as augmented reality (AR), virtual reality (VR), and interactive installations to create unique and memorable experiences. These innovations engage diners on multiple levels, stimulating their senses and enhancing the overall enjoyment of the meal. Immersive dining experiences blur the lines between food, art, and entertainment, offering a glimpse into the future of culinary creativity.

Sustainability will also play a crucial role in the future of dining. As consumers become more environmentally conscious, there is a growing demand for sustainable practices in the food industry. Farm-to-table initiatives, zero-waste restaurants, and plant-based dining options are just a few examples of how the industry is adapting to meet these demands. The focus on sustainability extends beyond the ingredients on the plate, encompassing the entire supply chain, from production to disposal. This shift towards sustainability reflects a broader cultural movement towards responsible consumption and environmental stewardship.

The integration of AI and robotics will continue to shape the future of dining experiences. AI-driven personalization will allow restaurants to tailor their offerings to individual preferences, creating bespoke dining experiences. Robotic chefs and servers will streamline operations and enhance efficiency, allowing human staff to focus on providing exceptional hospitality and service. The combination of human creativity and technological innovation will redefine the dining landscape, offering new opportunities for connection and interaction.

10

Chapter 10: The Role of Food in Community Building

Food has always been a powerful tool for building and strengthening communities. In this chapter, we explore how food fosters social bonds and creates a sense of belonging in various community settings.

Community gardens and urban farming initiatives have become popular ways for individuals to come together and grow their own food. These projects promote sustainability, self-sufficiency, and a connection to the land. By working side by side, community members build relationships and foster a sense of shared purpose. The produce grown in these gardens is often shared among participants or donated to local food banks, further strengthening the sense of community and mutual support.

Food cooperatives and community-supported agriculture (CSA) programs are other examples of how food can bring people together. These initiatives create a direct link between producers and consumers, fostering transparency, trust, and collaboration. By participating in a food cooperative or CSA, individuals contribute to the local economy, support sustainable farming practices, and gain access to fresh, high-quality produce. The communal aspect of these programs encourages members to engage with one another, share recipes, and learn about food production.

In addition to physical community-building efforts, digital platforms and online food communities have emerged as powerful tools for connection. Social media groups, food blogs, and virtual cooking classes provide opportunities for individuals to connect with like-minded people, share culinary experiences, and build relationships. These online communities transcend geographical boundaries, allowing individuals from different parts of the world to come together and celebrate their shared love of food. The sense of belonging and support found in these digital spaces highlights the enduring power of food to connect people, even in the digital age.

11

Chapter 11: Food and Emotional Well-being

The relationship between food and emotional well-being is complex and multifaceted. In this chapter, we explore how food can influence our emotions and contribute to mental health and happiness.

The act of eating is closely tied to emotional experiences. Comfort foods, for example, are often associated with positive memories and a sense of nostalgia. These foods can evoke feelings of happiness, security, and contentment, providing a temporary escape from stress and anxiety. On the other hand, certain foods can also have a negative impact on mood, leading to feelings of guilt or regret. Understanding the emotional significance of food can help individuals make more mindful choices and cultivate a healthier relationship with eating.

Nutritional neuroscience, a growing field of research, examines the impact of diet on brain function and mental health. Studies have shown that certain nutrients, such as omega-3 fatty acids, antioxidants, and vitamins, can influence mood and cognitive function. A balanced diet rich in these nutrients can support emotional well-being, reduce the risk of mental health disorders, and enhance overall quality of life. By recognizing the connection between diet and mental health, individuals can make informed choices that support their emotional and physical well-being.

Social aspects of eating also play a crucial role in emotional well-being. Shared meals provide opportunities for social interaction, fostering a sense of belonging and support. Regular family dinners, for example, have been linked to improved mental health outcomes in children and adolescents. The act of coming together around the table encourages open communication, strengthens relationships, and creates a supportive environment. By prioritizing shared meals, individuals can enhance their emotional well-being and build stronger social connections.

12

Chapter 12: Conclusion: Redefining Human Interaction Through Food

In the final chapter, we reflect on the themes explored throughout the book and consider how food continues to redefine human interaction in a rapidly changing world.

From its role in cultural exchange and community building to its impact on emotional well-being and technological innovation, food remains a powerful force for connection. It transcends geographical, cultural, and social barriers, fostering understanding, empathy, and collaboration. As we navigate the challenges and opportunities of the modern world, food serves as a reminder of our shared humanity and the importance of coming together.

The integration of technology, from AI and robotics to digital platforms, has introduced new dimensions to our relationship with food. These advancements have enhanced convenience, creativity, and personalization, offering exciting possibilities for the future of dining. At the same time, they remind us of the enduring significance of human connection and the need to balance innovation with tradition.

As we look to the future, the power of food to connect, inspire, and unite us will remain a central theme. By embracing the transformative potential of food, we can create a more inclusive, sustainable, and connected world. The recipe for connection lies in our ability to celebrate diversity, foster meaningful relationships, and recognize the profound impact of food on our lives and communities.

13

Chapter 13: The Role of Food in Education

Food serves as a valuable tool for education, fostering learning and development in various contexts. In this chapter, we explore how food can be used to teach important life skills, promote cultural awareness, and encourage healthy eating habits.

School gardens and farm-to-school programs are excellent examples of how food can enhance education. These initiatives provide hands-on learning experiences, allowing students to grow their own fruits and vegetables while learning about agriculture, nutrition, and sustainability. By engaging with the process of food production, students develop a deeper appreciation for the environment and gain practical skills that promote self-sufficiency and healthy eating.

Cooking classes and culinary education programs also play a crucial role in teaching essential life skills. By learning to cook, individuals acquire valuable knowledge about nutrition, meal planning, and food safety. These skills empower individuals to make informed dietary choices and cultivate a lifelong appreciation for good food. Culinary education programs also provide opportunities for social interaction and teamwork, fostering a sense of community and shared learning.

Cultural exchange programs that focus on food provide a unique opporttunity for students to learn about different culinary traditions and practices. These programs promote cultural awareness and appreciation, encouraging students to explore new flavors and cooking techniques. By sharing meals and recipes from around the world, students gain insights into the diverse ways that food shapes identity and fosters connection. The role of food in education highlights its potential to enrich learning experiences and promote a more inclusive and interconnected world.

14

Chapter 14: Food and Social Justice

Food plays a significant role in addressing social justice issues, from food insecurity and hunger to equitable access to healthy food. In this chapter, we examine how food can be a catalyst for positive change and social justice.

Food insecurity is a pressing issue that affects millions of people worldwide. Access to nutritious and affordable food is a fundamental human right, yet many individuals and communities face barriers to obtaining healthy food. Food banks, community kitchens, and meal assistance programs are essential resources that help address food insecurity and provide support to those in need. These initiatives rely on the generosity and collaboration of volunteers, donors, and organizations working together to ensure that everyone has access to adequate nutrition.

Equitable access to healthy food is another critical aspect of food justice. Food deserts, or areas with limited access to fresh and affordable produce, disproportionately affect low-income and marginalized communities. Efforts to address this issue include the establishment of farmers' markets, mobile grocery stores, and urban farming projects. By bringing fresh produce to underserved areas, these initiatives promote health equity and empower communities to take control of their food systems.

Culinary advocacy and activism also play a crucial role in advancing food justice. Chefs, food writers, and activists use their platforms to raise awareness about issues such as sustainable agriculture, fair labor practices, and food sovereignty. By highlighting the interconnectedness of food and social justice, these advocates inspire individuals to take action and contribute to a more equitable food system. The pursuit of food justice underscores the importance of collective efforts to create a fair and just world.

15

Chapter 15: The Impact of Food on Environmental Sustainability

The food industry has a significant impact on the environment, from resource consumption and waste production to greenhouse gas emissions. In this chapter, we explore how food choices and practices can contribute to environmental sustainability and mitigate climate change.

Sustainable agriculture practices aim to minimize the environmental footprint of food production. Techniques such as crop rotation, agroforestry, and organic farming promote soil health, biodiversity, and water conservation. By reducing the use of synthetic pesticides and fertilizers, sustainable agriculture practices protect ecosystems and enhance the resilience of food systems. Supporting sustainable farming practices and choosing sustainably produced food can help reduce the environmental impact of our diets.

Food waste is another critical issue that affects environmental sustainability. A significant portion of food produced globally is lost or wasted at various stages of the supply chain, from farm to table. Reducing food waste requires collective efforts, including improving storage and transportation infrastructure, implementing food recovery programs, and raising awareness about the importance of minimizing waste. By adopting practices such as meal planning, composting, and mindful consumption, individuals can contribute to reducing food waste and its environmental impact.

Plant-based diets have gained popularity as a means of promoting environmental sustainability. The production of plant-based foods generally requires fewer resources and generates lower greenhouse gas emissions compared to animal-based foods. By incorporating more plant-based options into their diets, individuals can reduce their ecological footprint and support a more sustainable food system. The impact of food on environmental sustainability highlights the importance of making conscious food choices and supporting practices that protect the planet.

16

Chapter 16: The Role of Food in Health and Wellness

Food plays a central role in promoting health and wellness, influencing physical, mental, and emotional well-being. In this chapter, we explore how food can be used to support a healthy lifestyle and prevent chronic diseases.

A balanced diet rich in essential nutrients is the foundation of good health. Consuming a variety of fruits, vegetables, whole grains, lean proteins, and healthy fats provides the body with the nutrients it needs to function optimally. Nutritional guidelines and dietary recommendations emphasize the importance of incorporating these nutrient-dense foods into daily meals. By making informed dietary choices, individuals can support their overall health and reduce the risk of chronic diseases such as heart disease, diabetes, and obesity.

Functional foods and superfoods have gained attention for their potential health benefits. These foods are rich in bioactive compounds, such as antioxidants, vitamins, and minerals, that have been shown to support various aspects of health. For example, foods like blueberries, turmeric, and quinoa are known for their anti-inflammatory and immune-boosting properties. Incorporating functional foods into the diet can enhance health and wellness, providing additional support for the body's natural processes.

The connection between food and mental health is also an important consideration. Nutritional psychiatry is a growing field that examines the impact of diet on mood, cognitive function, and mental health. Studies have shown that certain nutrients, such as omega-3 fatty acids, B vitamins, and magnesium, can support brain health and reduce the risk of mental health disorders. By prioritizing a diet rich in these nutrients, individuals can promote mental well-being and enhance their overall quality of life.

17

Chapter 17: The Future of Food and Society

As we look to the future, the relationship between food and society will continue to evolve, influenced by technological advancements, cultural shifts, and global challenges. In this chapter, we explore the future of food and its potential to shape human interaction and societal development.

Technological innovations will play a significant role in the future of food production and consumption. Advances in biotechnology, such as lab-grown meat and cellular agriculture, have the potential to revolutionize the way we produce protein and reduce the environmental impact of animal agriculture. These innovations offer promising solutions to address food security and sustainability while meeting the growing demand for protein-rich foods.

The rise of personalized nutrition is another exciting trend in the future of food. Advances in genetic research and AI-driven analytics enable the development of customized dietary recommendations based on an individual's unique genetic makeup, lifestyle, and health goals. Personalized nutrition has the potential to enhance health outcomes and prevent chronic diseases by tailoring dietary interventions to individual needs. This approach reflects a growing recognition of the importance of individualized care and the potential of data-driven insights to improve well-being.

Global challenges such as climate change, population growth, and resource scarcity will shape the future of food and society. Addressing these challenges requires innovative solutions and collaborative efforts across sectors. Sustainable food systems, circular economy practices, and resilient supply chains will be essential to ensure food security and environmental sustainability. By embracing these principles and working together, we can create a future where food continues to connect, nourish, and inspire us.

Book Description: "The Recipe for Connection: How Food, Society, and Robots Redefine Human Interaction"

In a world where technology and tradition often seem at odds, "The Recipe for Connection" explores the profound ways in which food bridges the gap between the two, creating new avenues for human interaction. This engaging and thought-provoking book delves into the timeless power of food to connect people across cultures, foster community, and inspire innovation.

Through twelve captivating chapters, the book examines the social dynamics of dining, the role of food in cultural exchange, and the impact of technology on culinary practices. From the communal tables of ancient civilizations to the rise of virtual dinner parties and AI-driven dining experiences, the narrative highlights how food remains a central force in shaping our relationships and identities.

Readers will discover how robots and artificial intelligence are revolutionizing the food industry, enhancing efficiency and creativity while preserving the essence of human connection. The book also addresses pressing issues such as food justice, sustainability, and the role of food in emotional well-being, offering insights into how we can create a more inclusive and resilient food system.

"The Recipe for Connection" is a celebration of food's unique ability to transcend boundaries and bring people together. It invites readers to explore the rich tapestry of human interaction through the lens of food, technology, and society, ultimately revealing the universal truth that food is more than sustenance—it's a powerful medium for connection and transformation.

www.ingramcontent.com/pod-product-compliance
Lightning Source LLC
LaVergne TN
LVHW010442070526
838199LV00066B/6139